Now What?

A Beginner's Guide to Living Saved

Nicole Brown

iUniverse, Inc.
New York   Bloomington

iUniverse books may be ordered through booksellers or by contacting:

iUniverse
1663 Liberty Drive
Bloomington, IN 47403
www.iuniverse.com
1-800-Authors (1-800-288-4677)

ISBN: 978-1-4401-6528-3 (sc)
ISBN: 978-1-4401-6527-6 (ebook)

Printed in the United States of America

Library of Congress Control Number: 2009934577

iUniverse rev. date: 09/24/2009

Table of Contents

Introduction

I would like to begin by saying that a year ago it was not my intent to write a book. Even more to the point, it was never my intent to write a book about helping others get closer to God. So why am I writing this? Well, I was in the middle of church one day, and our pastor was urging us to ask God what we could do for His Kingdom. To "take our walk to the next level" is really what our pastor asked us to ask God. When I got home I began to pray, and I told God that I was ready for whatever assignment He had for me. I did not receive a reply right away; it was days later when I was driving to work that God answered. He clearly showed me a book that I was going to write, and this book was going to help others with their Christian walk. The premise for the book should be "What to Expect When You're Expecting" meets "Christianity for Dummies," He said.

I must say, at first I was not eager to embark on this assignment. I put it off and put it off until the urge to write it became so compelling I just had to begin taking notes and developing the structure. During this process, I was still not convinced that writing this book was something that I should be doing. "God," I said, "even if I wrote this book, who would read it? Even more important, who would buy it?" He answered, "Why not you?" It was so profound in its simplicity. Throughout God's word, He shows us that anyone can be used to do great things. He used a prostitute named Rahab to hide the two spies when going to investigate Jericho for Joshua (Joshua 2:1). Later in her life,

3

Rahab gave birth to one of Jesus's forefathers, Boaz (Matthew 1:5). This is when I began to reflect on my life and really think about why God was choosing me to do this for Him.

When I was twelve, I accepted Jesus into my life for the first time. I believe that I have done this at least five times since then. When I was a fledgling Christian, there was no one who took the time to lead and guide me. No one told me what to expect from this newfound salvation. I did not know that there were promises for me in the Bible. I really did not know that Satan targets those who are saved and have a purpose in the Kingdom of God— every Christian. I guess everyone I knew, took for granted that God leads his believers. Looking back now, I really wish I had someone who took the time to pull me to the side and at least lay the groundwork for my Christian walk. Alas, there I was, a baby Christian flung from my nest without so much as a feather in my wings. I was walking into unknown territory without any of the tools I needed to survive.

The fact that I had no idea how to be a Christian was evident. I am now on my third marriage, and I have six beautiful children. If someone had told me that God offered all the love I needed, I may not have been looking for love in places that I was sure not to find it. I know, without a doubt, that if I had had a Christian support system, I never would have opened the door of divorce into my life. And I would have understood that when God gives us a test and we fail, we have to take the test over and over and over until we finally pass it. After my second divorce, I began to seek a deeper relationship with God. I began reading my Bible and praying, but I was still living in the Christian world by myself. I felt that now I was on the Christian road, I was doing everything right, and I misunderstood that God needed to work changes in me and not everyone else around me. God rescued me from depression, poverty, and physical and mental abuse, yet I still did not understand why or how to really live like a Christian. I knew that there was something I was missing, but I was still unsure what that something was.

It was not until marriage number three that I finally conceded to letting God have full control. Mind you, this marriage has been a roller coaster of mammoth proportions, but I see the changes that God has made in me, finally. I entered this marriage as a new person in Christ, and I was bound and determined not to let failure take claim of another marriage. This has been much easier said than done. We battle big demons over here in my camp. In marriage one, I faced adultery and verbal abuse. In marriage number two, there was adulterous behavior and also physical and verbal abuse. Now in marriage number three, we have been battling many types of abuse with a side order of addiction and incarceration. Remember, I told you that if we fail the test we have to go through it again. Well, what I neglected to mention is that when we go through the test again, we are usually faced with compounded issues and problems. I must also mention that it is not God who tempts us. Satan perverts God's test in order to get us off our path. Oh, and I could not blame God for all the abuse and so on because this is all behavior that comes from demons and sin, not God.

I know what you must be thinking: if she is going through these things, why does she stay in the marriage? I have an answer for that. I did not really make the vow to my husband; I made the vow to God, and I will either trust Him to honor His word or I will not. Not trusting Him didn't get me very far, so I have to do this the right way and trust Him. Too often we think that if we just get out of the situation and start over, it will be much better next time. We are so wrong; as you have seen, we still have to go through the test. Now the players may be different, but the game is still the same until we pass. God has grown me from a meek, depressed, unsure woman into a bold fighting woman of God. The funny thing is that when I was young, I was confident, and sure, Satan and life beat that out of me, but God was so faithful that He not only restored my confidence and sanity, He also cleared the cobwebs and allowed my mind to be creative and thoughtful again. Staying in God's presence and doing what He asks is not for others as much as it is for me.

When I married my third husband five years ago, I had some saved friends, but when things began looking crazy, I started to falter again. Now, I was going to college, I knew that I wanted to be a psychologist and that God was leading me in this direction to help people with addictions. So, I was working a full-time job, caring for my husband and six children, and going to school full time, and if that wasn't stressful enough, things in my marriage were getting worse, by the day, I was sure we were losing the battle of addiction, and *helpless* is not a powerful enough word to describe how I felt. Then, there it was: after a huge episode with my husband, I received a call from a friend. She invited her pastor's wife to pray with us; at the end of the conversation, I felt it, belonging. That feeling when you know the pieces of the puzzle have come together and you can get comfortable. I went to their church on that same Sunday and the rest is history. God led me to people who understood that this walk is not easy. These were people who were honest about their shortcomings and were not afraid to share and help you through anything. The pastor and his wife really take my walk, with God, personally. They truly understand what a shepherd is and what his job is regarding his flock. For the first time in my Christian walk I was receiving guidance and learning how to be a good Christian. They began answering all my lifelong questions and now I could finally understand where I had missed God's point so many times. Finally, I was able to deal with life's issues. I had the support I needed to move on and really spread my Christian wings.

The work that God has done in me is nothing short of amazing. I have gone from pessimist to optimist. From closed and detached to outwardly loving. God is working on my marriage, but He had to work on me first. I no longer shudder at the first sign of adversity. I stand fast and pray when I really need to let God know I will be faithful to Him just like He is faithful to me. The way I look at me has changed, the way I look at others has changed, and the way I deal with situations has changed. Is everything perfect? Not at all, but I now have the tools and the knowledge to deal with what Satan tries to throw at me. Don't get me wrong, there are still times that I question my purpose and this path, but I now have to tools to get past these brief periods and push through to the other side.

This book is an important work to me. I really tried to capture the essence of all the things that I struggled with in the beginning of my walk with God. I included a story about my experiences in each chapter so you could see where I learned the lesson. I wanted readers to have a tool that they could use to help them, in the beginning of their Christian life. On these pages you will find answers to some very important questions you may have about God and your walk with Him. I chose issues that every new Christian will have to deal with from the moment they accept Jesus into their heart. Think of this as the hand on your shoulder or the big sister giving you the talk about the birds and the bees. Guidance is necessary to be a successful Christian and I hope that this book gives you the direction that you will need to be an *Overcomer* in Christ's kingdom. When you read this, know that I have been right where you are now, and all my scrapes and bruises are worth it if this helps you in any way.

Chapter 1: Be Prepared from Day One

From the day you accept the Lord into your heart, there is joy and jubilation. You have started a journey that will lead you to the Promised Land. All your pain will end, all of your troubles will disintegrate, and by the way, there will be a "New to the Kingdom of God" check in the mail when you get home. Can this be true? I am here to tell you, yes and no. Yes, you will reap blessings, unimaginable blessings, and you have found a place in the Kingdom of Heaven. The answer is no in the fact that you will have to work; you will have to work harder than you have ever had to work at anything in your entire life. Any married person will tell you that marriage takes work, and they are not lying. As a matter of fact, all relationships require work to sustain a pleasant and meaningful bond. God has diligently been working for you, and when you become born again, your part of the work begins, even though you have no idea what type of work is expected of you.

The important thing to remember about salvation is that you were bought for a price. Salvation came to you through the sacrifice of Jesus Christ, and only by this sacrifice can you be free. However, it is always beneficial to read the fine print. Not many people recite their acceptance-of-Jesus speech and leave with a *What to Expect When You Have Accepted Jesus as Your Lord and Savior* book. On the contrary, many people leave the sanctuary skipping and Holy Ghost filled only to find that sin and disappointment are still waiting in the car for the ride home. Many find this so discouraging that their fledgling faith is left by the roadside only a few miles away from the church and the fear of choosing to walk that narrow walk again is now overwhelming. Fortunately for us, God does not hold us in condemnation, and we have endless opportunities to seek Him and all His Glory.

> "Many people leave the sanctuary skipping and Holy Ghost–filled only to find that sin and disappointment are still waiting in the car for the ride home."

The first rule of salvation is to be prepared. Satan has not taken a vacation because you decided to give your life over to Christ. In fact, you were far less interesting when you were not saved. Think about it: you handed Satan a gun, kicked him in the shin, and ran away, slowly. Don't believe for one minute that you have not been appointed tops on his "people to destroy" list. Oh, and for the record, as you grow in God's ministry, find your purpose, and become more Christlike, the enemy begins thinking of new and exciting ways to come against you. Fear not, though; God's word says that "No weapon formed against you shall prosper" (Isaiah 54:17). This means that as long as you remain close to God and are constantly growing in the Spirit, you will remain victorious. Suffice it to say, anything worth having is worth working hard for, and I believe that an eternity in the Lord's presence without sickness, debt, or death is one of those things worth having.

So, how do you prepare for what is coming? (And make no mistake about it, it is coming.) Get your handy-dandy Bible and a concordance, and if you have Internet access to use a search engine like (www.google.com) to look up your Bible based questions, that is even better. (All the Bible quotes, in this book, have been taken from the NIV version of the Bible.) Begin asking questions and looking up scriptures that pertain to your personal issues and situations. What is your job description? What are the benefits of this job? Most importantly, what are the requirements of this job and what are the rules of this company in which I have newly become employed? Think about it; have you ever started a job without knowing when you would be paid and what benefits this company offers, let alone what was expected of you? I think not. In the world we ask questions about things we hear about, see in movies, and read in books. Why is it so difficult to ask questions about the most important journey you will ever embark upon? "The road is narrow" (Matthew 7:14) and you will be better off if you are fully prepared for your walk.

You also want to stay in church; this is your support system and believe me, you will need people around you who you can trust. In the book of Romans, the Apostle Paul talks about how important the church is. He later says that "Jesus Himself is returning for His Church that will be without spot, wrinkle or blemish" (Ephesians 5:27). Is he looking for you and your church? If you are not rooted in a good church family, it may be difficult for you to grow spiritually, especially if you are new at this. It may be difficult for you to remain

Find a good Church home with people who are willing to guide you, be honest with you, and stand with you through any situation.

spot and blemish free. Consider this; not only do computers come with instruction manuals, they also come with technical support, and we could all use some technical support from time to time. Who will pray for you when you are weak, who will guide you and help you enter into the presence of the Lord? Still another reason to remain in church is the rule that "One can set a thousand to flight, but 2 can set ten thousand to flight" (Deuteronomy 32:30). If this is the rule, then imagine how many obstacles you can overcome with more than two people standing in agreement with you; the possibilities are endless.

When I was new to the Christian world, I was on my own. I had a Bible and I went to church, but there was no one to take me by the hand and lead me in the right direction. I really suffered for this throughout my life. I did not understand that Satan wanted to destroy me, my family, and everyone I came in contact with. I have suffered through, divorce, depression, confusion, abuse, disobedience both in me and my children, chaos, and a multitude of other gifts from the kingdom of darkness. When I finally read my Bible, I really did not know that I was supposed to pray and ask God for His guidance in understanding the scripture. However, I was also wrong in assuming that because I was reading my Bible and praying that I now was completely healed, whole, and delivered and everyone else needed help from God so that they could line up with my thinking.

I have since learned, through my support system, that reading and praying is was not enough. I needed to be prepared for Satan's attacks. Even more importantly, I needed to know that God had promises for me and my life and Satan would use any means to try and steal these promises from me. The funny thing about this is when I did not know that Satan was targeting me, I began freely giving him my power and authority because there was no one in my corner to teach me how to avoid this costly mistake. Now, I am blessed with people who will stand with me, pray with me, and teach me the difference between being saved and living saved. I have seen God move and change situations with the simplest prayer and I have seen him move mountains in me. Anyone can have a successful walk with God if they find people who are honest and willing to put down themselves in the interest of guiding others.

My advice to you is to find a church family where you can be yourself and your faith can be given an opportunity to grow. I am here to tell you that they do exist. You may have to search, but when you find the right place you will know it in your heart, and these people will become your family.

The last part of preparation would be to get your Bible, and for heaven's sake read it *all*. Seriously, actually pick up your Bible, turn the pages, and read it. This is not a coffee-table book to be placed in the center of your table with the intent of being used as a clever coaster for your tea party guests. It is not a paperweight or a flyswatter and it will not plug the rust hole in your trunk. Use your Bible for studying the word; it is a learning tool intended to be used by you. Take notes at every opportunity: during service, at Bible study, and even when you are reading on your own. I know the pages are pristine and delicate, so write gently, but Mark It Up! And if you are self-conscious about all your scribbling, get a second Bible for when company comes. Oh, and by the way, it is not doing you any good keeping it in your car so you don't forget to bring it to service. News flash: every church has extra Bibles just in case you leave yours on the bedside table. I know it can seem difficult to remember your Bible at first, but the first steps are always the hardest.

Note:

* Don't ever take anyone's word for it; always look it up for yourself.
* Use this book to take notes and then come back in a few months and look at your progress.

Chapter Questions:

Day I was born again

_____

Scriptures I am interested in learning

_____
_____
_____
_____
_____

Questions for my pastor _____

_____
_____
_____
_____
_____
_____

Preparation I will take for my walk with God _____

_____
_____
_____
_____
_____

Notes:

Chapter 2: Know Your Enemy

Satan will come! Are you surprised? Now, that you have been walking with God, you may be comfortable. Ask yourself this, who have I really helped while I have remained here, in my comfort zone? What kind of differences have I made? Remember when you were a new Christian and donned the big white T-shirt with the red bull's-eye painted on it (you know the one), then you handed Satan the crossbow? Well, when you became complacent he has seemingly backed off. But we need to change the way we think. We need to use our offensive plays and keep him on the run. This will not come without challenge, though. Once you begin moving in God's direction and begin operating in what God desires from you, you will get noticed.

> "Once you begin moving in God's direction and begin operating in what God desires from you, you will get noticed.."

Imagine being at a deliverance session and you are praying with the tools the Lord has possessed you with. Now, you get home and all of a sudden all hell has broken loose in your children; they are workin' your last nerve, and your response is, for lack of a better reference, to get a little Old Testament on that behind. Where did this come from? First, you stepped out of your comfort zone and prayed for others, and now you have to battle all this craziness in your home. Why? Because you made a difference. You caused a ripple in the otherwise calm of the world. Did you think that this would come without attack? You must be prepared for the fact that when you begin to operate in what God wants, the enemy is on the move to deter your efforts at any cost. Maybe he can even keep you from doing that ever again; after all that is his goal.

I remember the first day I attended church at Living Word. I was overcome by the urge to let them know that I could sing. I told them that I would be interested in singing for the church, and they asked to hear me. Needless to say, I got the job. The next week, I was singing in the church, just like that. My kids were all there and I was beaming with pride because it felt so right. Not five minutes after we left the church, the kids were immediately on their worst behavior. They were yelling and screaming in the back of the van. They would not calm down; I was instantly frustrated. Immediately after we arrived home, my husband and I started arguing. There was anger throughout the house and everyone was yelling. The kids were crying and throwing things. I did not understand that I was under attack for what I had done. I never thought that I would experience these kinds of repercussions from twenty minutes of praise and worship singing. The remainder of the week was horrible. Car problems, constant arguments, and disobedience were the least of the problems I experienced that week. I was so frustrated that I did not want to go in for praise and worship practice the next Saturday, and I certainly was in no mood to sing on Sunday. He did it, Satan kept me from doing that again, or so he thought. Thank God for my pastor's wife. She explained to me that I was under attack for stepping forward and walking in what God had for me. She explained to me that Satan was angry and would stop at nothing until I was deterred from my purpose. To tell you the truth, this made me angry. How dare you try to wreak havoc in my life? From that point on I decided I was not going down without a fight and I would not let Satan keep me from God's plan and purpose for my life. Not only did I sing the next week, I continued to sing every week until God moved me on.

What you need to realize is that Satan has studied you since before you were born and he has the mind realm at his disposal for all of the people who are closest to you. Fortunately for you, Satan cannot use anything that is foreign to you as a weapon against you. God's word says that "No temptation has seized you except what is common to man. And God is faithful; he will not let you be tempted beyond what you can bear. But when you are tempted, he will also provide a way out so that you can stand up under it" (1 Corinthians 10:13). This means that Satan has rules that are governed by God Almighty and he cannot come against you with anything you are not familiar with. Now look at what God does for you in return: not only will He not let you be tempted past what you can bear, but He will also offer you a way out of every situation. How great is that? Tests and trials make us stronger, but when the enemy comes with temptation, God has already given us an escape route.

Remember, you are also protected by the armor of God:

Finally, be strong in the Lord and in his mighty power. Put on the full armor of God so that you can take your stand against the devil's schemes. For our struggle is not against flesh and blood, but against the rulers, against the authorities, against the powers of this dark world and against the spiritual forces of evil in the heavenly realms. Therefore put on the full armor of God, so that when the day of evil comes, you may be able to stand your ground, and after you have done everything, to stand. Stand firm then, with the belt of truth buckled around your waist, with the breastplate of righteousness in place, and with your feet fitted with the readiness that comes from the gospel of peace. In addition to all this, take up the shield of faith, with which you can extinguish all the flaming arrows of the evil one. Take the helmet of salvation and the sword of the Spirit, which is the word of God. And pray in the Spirit on all occasions with all kinds of prayers and requests. With this in mind, be alert and always keep on praying for all the saints.

(Ephesians 6:10–18).

God has given you this armor so you can stand facing your enemy, pushing forward, offensively moving until your enemy flees or is destroyed. Retaliation comes, though; Satan can turn trials and tests into temptations. Even Jesus was subjected to Satan's tricks when he tried to tempt Jesus in the desert (Matthew 4:1–10). Satan uses enticing little tidbits that can knock even the strongest Christian off his mark. For example, take that sin that you were really good at, in the world. You know the one that is your weakness and when Satan comes to exploit it, you are ready to fight head-on , but watch your side because as you are turning away from one temptation you may just wind up smack dab in the middle of another. We must be well versed in the tricks of the enemy, and we must be well grounded in the Word. Satan can only lead us if we are willing to go, and he will only flee if we submit to God and resist him (James 4:7).

Don't forget that every step you take toward God's kingdom is creating discomfort for Satan and his minions. Each time you resist Satan, you become stronger. Every word that you read enhances your relationship with God, and Satan is mad about it. The enemy is determined to destroy you and everyone around you. Oh, and don't forget, if you have become strong enough to resist the devil, he will go after those close to you. He is the king of darkness and the father of lies. He has turned manipulation into an art form. Who do you think writes for the soaps? (Kidding.) You have to rely on God's word to lead and guide you. God will grant you wisdom, strength, and perseverance if you are strong enough to ask.

Note:

Even Jesus did not rebuke Satan. The proper rebuke would be, "Satan the Lord rebuke you." However, it is important to remember that God's word says "Resist the devil and he will flee" (James 4:7), so really, all we have to do is resist and pray for guidance.

Chapter Questions:

How will I resist temptations? _____
_____
_____
_____
_____

How can I strengthen my weaknesses? _____
_____
_____
_____
_____
_____
_____

Scriptures that will help me when I feel weak _____
_____
_____
_____
_____
_____
_____

Notes:

_____
_____
_____
_____
_____
_____
_____
_____
_____
_____
_____
_____
_____
_____
_____
_____
_____
_____
_____
_____
_____
_____
_____
_____
_____
_____
_____
_____

Chapter 3: Get New Friends.

In the word, you will hear much talk about a yoke; please note that it is not a *yolk*—you cannot bake with it or make omelets. The word says, "Do not be yoked together with unbelievers. For what do righteousness and wickedness have in common? Or, what fellowship can light have with darkness?" (2 Corinthians 6:14). So, what does it really mean to be evenly yoked with someone? Well, yoke has several definitions, so I will try to make it easier to understand. Say you have two oxen pulling a cart;

> *The Bible warns against being yoked with unbelievers*

one is very small and weak, and the other is big and strong. When they are pulling the load it is not evenly dispersed because they are not evenly yoked. Now, one of two things has to happen: either the larger ox does more work or he slows down to the level of the smaller ox. The same principle holds true for the yoking of people in God's Kingdom. If you are not on the same level as those around you, they have the potential to bring you right back down into the life that you are trying so hard to change and maybe even leave behind. This scripture is very important in the choosing of a husband or wife, but it is also important to remember that even friendships require an even yoking when you are on a quest for righteousness.

Now, when you are first saved there are some friends who

will be supportive and even encouraging and there will be some who appreciate the gossip fodder that you have just supplied them with. By the way, you should be good for a healthy bout of ridicule and laughter for days and maybe even weeks to come. These are people who have watched you do things that may have been sinful and even downright dirty. "Here you come now; are you going to ride in all holier than thou, on your high horse and try to preach your own salvation? Please, if I remember correctly, you were the one shakin' it on the dance floor with a drink in one hand and a member of the opposite sex in the other, just two weeks ago. Now, here you are all Saint (Insert your name here) today, and I don't buy it." No matter what the words are, the sentiment is always the same. The hardest critics of your salvation are those people who you considered closest to you. This is another reason why a good church family is so important. You will need support; and the worst thing for you, right now, is seeking guidance from those who are not supportive of your walk with God.

Several years ago I was trying to sort out my new walk with God. I did not know anything, so I found myself looking to those around me who were "seasoned Christians." Looking back now, I understand that "seasoned" and "Christian" do not necessarily belong together. The idea was that we would live our lives however we wanted during the week and when Sunday came we would have our bodies in church so that we could be forgiven for all our sins. There was always a production of "falling out" in the Spirit after a lengthy sermon that told us we would be forgiven no matter what we did, which gave the impression that it was okay to sin and then ask for forgiveness. During the week, between Sundays, a whole multitude of things went on: backbiting, gossip, partying, fornication. You name it, it was being done, all in the name of living a saved life.

Advice was always contrary to the Word and it became a lifestyle that proclaimed, as long as I don't kill anyone, I am okay in God's eyes. We always seemed to have fun, but it was an illusion. There was no trust and a severe lack of self-confidence, and money was not exactly growing on trees. I even remember being coaxed into the club, all based on the fear that if I did not go I would be talked about and ridiculed by those closest to me. We all seemed to be content with this shell of an unsatisfying life we were leading. It was horrible. You should never be in a situation where you are constantly leery of the people you call your friends. I had to take some time off. I knew, deep inside, that if I wanted to really get closer to God, this was not the way to do it. This could not really be all that God promised in His word. I began to move away and was often called uppity or a number of other terms that were not very flattering. It was difficult. These were people who had been key components, in my life, for years. We did everything together and now I knew that this was not where I needed to be. The transition was hard, since I didn't have that many friends to begin with. I did, however, happen to be blessed with three women who I can truly call my friends, three women who have seen me through the hard times while remaining consistent, Godly influences. They are now my sisters, because "friend" does not describe their role with enough justice.

This walk can be difficult enough without the constant badgering of people who do not have your best interest at heart. Don't get me wrong. Some people will support you. Others will try to pull you back in to your old life and others will fall by the wayside, never to be heard from again. There is a song entitled "Stand" by John P.

> *"Through this walk you will be required to stand for what is right in God's eyes not what is right in the eyes of the world"*

Kee, and the words are actually quite profound. He says, "I decided to take a stand not knowing I would lose my best friends, but I would rather, rather live right than burn in Hell lift up my eyes." Sometimes you will feel like you are losing the people around you and things that you want or need, but is it really worth missing out on your salvation? Through this walk you will be required to stand. To stand for God and what is right in His eyes, not what is right in the eyes of this world.

Take heart, dear one, you will not be alone. God has made provisions for you, this I guarantee. He will send you people, people who are evenly yoked with you; people, who began their new life at the altar, just like you; people who believe that this walk is the best thing that they have ever undertaken. He will send you loving friends who are understanding and kind. You need the kind of people who will garner you with Godly advice and not the people who will say, "Girl, you got to go and get away from this nonsense" or "Man, leave all that alone." Believe me, you will know the Godly advice from the un-Godly advice immediately, even though many times the un-Godly advice will sound much better to your flesh. Seek out people who take their walk with God seriously, people who will pray for you any hour of the day or night, even in the middle of dinner at your favorite restaurant. You can call them friend, but eventually you will call them brothers and sisters in Christ. They will become your family, your support, and your friends.

By the way, Satan will use whosoever he can to try to bring you to ruin and he can manipulate anyone, not walking with God, into being a thorn in your side. Don't let him knock you down. He is under your feet and not the other way around. You have mighty tools at your disposal and you need to use them. Read, pray, and get to know people who love you and support you no matter what you have done in the past or in your future. These are going to be the people who will help you when you need it the most. Trust me, I've been there, done that, and bought the T-shirt, and now I wouldn't trade in any of my sisters for all the sin in the world.

Chapter Questions:

Who is a Godly influence?

_____
_____
_____
_____
_____

Who is not a Godly influence?

_____
_____
_____
_____

Prayer for friends who are not Godly friends

_____
_____
_____
_____
_____

People I can stand and agree with

_____
_____
_____
_____
_____

Notes:

Chapter 4: Give Up the World

Okay, here's the score; you were saved on Sunday and today, the following Saturday, Friday? Oh, who am I kidding? It is probably Wednesday and your newfound salvation is about to interfere with your *old* flesh. It begins with one phone call, you know, from one of the friends on your list in chapter 3. She calls, like usual, with the hottest invitation to the hottest place with the hottest people. Who can resist? (Guys, you know you have these friends too.) YOU CAN RESIST!! And you have to resist for your own sake. I know that it has not been long since you let Jesus into your heart, but Satan comes quickly to destroy what God has for you, so you need to be on your guard. Believe me, there is nothing tastier to the Prince of Persia (Daniel, 10:13) than a newly saved Christian. Right now is the time when you will have to make a concerted effort to leave those bad habits behind you, far behind you.

I mean honestly, how much fun was it really? Do you even remember what you did when the party was over? Are you happy with what you did when the party was over? Who wants to remember all that? I don't know how many times I have heard the same story; got lifted, looked like a blubbering idiot while

> "By Wednesday, your new found salvation is about to interfere with your old flesh"

running around the bar before trying to drive home while the road was spinning, or better yet I just woke up next to some random guy who well, let's face it, if I wasn't so drunk I don't think I would have let him buy me the whole bar, let alone go home with him and get into bed.

It is the time to make a conscious decision to leave the old world back there in puking-up-my-guts-and-making-poor-choices land. I am not saying you have to go cold turkey, but think about this: if I put beer in a glass, it will never be anything but beer. No matter what you do or where you take it, if you put beer into the glass you will get beer out. It is time to begin filling your glass with God; that means Jesus, the Holy Ghost, the Bible, and anything else Kingdom approved. We are not of this world, so how can we participate in worldly activities and expect to be in the right standing with God? I think that many people believe that if they get themselves saved they can no longer have any fun; this is so not true! Your idea of fun just changes. I did not change everything overnight, but I did notice that once I began to make changes to my world, it became easier to make more changes one at a time, step by step. One thing to note is that in order to be a successful follower of Christ, you will need to make it your goal to change *everything* that is not Godly in your life. This will not be an overnight thing; it will take time and dedication to change, and you are so worth it!

Here are some easy steps to ensure conversion success.

Music: Find a station that plays Christian music that is similar to your music of choice. I would not suggest listening to the light Christian station if your musical preference is rap. This could be a road to disaster. There are many resources on the Internet that can help you locate your Christian music genre. Begin slowly trying different music until you find some that you like. Soon, you will be listening to Christian music full-time. You may even find your old music difficult to listen to, even painful, at times.

As you learned previously, from the first Sunday I attended I began to sing there, during praise and worship service. I was also asked to perform some pieces by myself. I was really unfamiliar with the music. My music genre was R&B; I knew absolutely nothing about gospel and Christian music except for a select few songs I knew from the Sister Act movies. I was convinced that this was what God had for me to do, so I asked my girlfriend, the music encyclopedia, if she had any suggestions. Turns out she did; some of it I liked and some of it I didn't. I began looking on the Internet at gospel music sites and found a wealth of information regarding artists and music. I got my hands on as much music as I could. Now, we are a musical family, from my husband to my children. We all enjoyed the same kinds of music, until now. I was about to embark into uncharted territory. At first, I only looked for music that I would be able to sing in church. I made a couple of CDs and began listening in the car. Not much had changed. We would listen to the worldly music when we were all together, but when I was by myself I found I was listening less to the radio and more to these CDs.

Then it happened, I am not sure when or how, but it most definitely happened. I was no longer able to tolerate worldly music. I mean it was so repulsive to me that I would get an instant headache. This is when my husband chose to venture into the new school, down south rap category. I hated it. I found myself getting offended at all the F-bombs and the other profanity. I even started noticing how degrading it was to women. Wow, I was a prude! That's what he thought. He did not understand how I could no longer listen to all of this. I even started asking him not to play it in front of the children. When he and I would ride together, in the car, I would listen to my MP3 player because even though he liked some gospel, it seemed that the more I embraced it the more he couldn't tolerate it. Now, we all listen to gospel music; it brings a calm over our entire household. In fact, when things seem a little chaotic, I will turn on the music and watch the atmosphere change, instantly.

Activities: There are alternatives to the things that you used to do. Instead of meeting at the club and shakin' your tail feather till the morn, meet at a sports bar or even a restaurant. Try to find some place you can meet people that does not revolve around alcohol or booty shakin'. This may take time, but the less of Satan you invite into your life, the easier your walk will be; it is

> *Christians are not of this world; therefore we must live like we are not of this world.*

up to you. Who knows, you might find that being conscious during activities makes them more enjoyable, and you could even digest your meal instead of wearing it on your favorite shoes. (I know I am not the only one who has told this story!)

Cursing: I have included an entire chapter on guarding what comes out of your mouth, so this section will be brief. In the word it says that "out of the overflow of the heart the mouth speaks" (Matthew 12:34). That means that if you are constantly cursing, and in case you were confused, that is what all those fun four-letter words are, curses. If you are constantly cursing, you are really harming yourself and showing God that this is what is in your heart. I don't think this is truly why you asked God to come into your life, is it?

Bad Habits: When it comes to bad habits—smoking, overeating, etc—we may need some additional help. Deliverance is something that you should discuss with your pastor in order to decide if it is really what you need. However, do not ever underestimate the power of prayer. When you begin to make changes in your life, your bad habits may put up some resistance, but his word says that "Greater is He that is in me than he that is in the world" (1

John 4:4). Do you believe you serve a mighty God, that He has the power to change all things? Then trust Him to do it for you.

I know that you can do this; remember, God knows you and he does not expect you to change an entire lifetime of worldly living in one day. You will fall, but the true measure of your faith comes when you get back up, dust yourself off, and continue on your path. "Submit yourselves, then to God. Resist the devil and he will flee from you" (James 4:7). It works: when you submit and resist Satan backs off, he cannot stand against God's power, remember that. Soon, you will be looking back at where you came from and when you see how far you have grown, you will be amazed.

Chapter Questions:

God, what would you have me change first? _____

_____

_____

_____

_____

Steps I will take to successful change _____

_____

_____

_____

_____

Who will be my support system?

_____

_____

_____

_____

_____

What if I fall?

_____

_____

_____

_____

_____

Notes:

Chapter 5: Faith

What is faith? This is the first question that you should know the answer to. The second question you should know the answer to is, why is faith important? Not only should you know the answers to these questions; you should know how to apply faith in your life. Faith in Hebrews 11:1 reads "Now faith is the substance of things that are hoped for, the evidence of things not seen." Faith is something that is not tangible; it is real. It is something that you just know. Jesus had faith; every Gospel tells of his faith in

> "Are you willing to step out on faith and do whatever it is that God is asking of you?"

God's plan for his life. He stepped out on faith in order to fulfill his Father's wishes even though it meant his physical torture and death. Are you willing to step out on faith to do whatever it is that God wishes for you to do? Are you willing to let God lead your life no matter what your eyes see? This is faith. Everyone has a measure of faith when they become born-again Christians. Jesus said all God needs is for you to have a mustard seed's worth of faith to move mountains, but God provides you with so much more faith than that (Matthew 17:20).

Faith has to be very important since Jesus mentions it often. When you are reading Matthew, Mark, Luke, or John you see how Jesus is constantly making references to the faith of his disciples, or lack thereof. The Roman centurion (Matthew 8:5–13) and the "woman with the issue of blood" (Luke 8:43–48) both had faith enough for healing to occur in their lives and the lives of those they loved. Jesus made it a point to mention these marks of faith to his entourage; he was amazed at the faith of those who did not follow him as compared to those who did. Jesus took time to reprimand his disciples for their lack of faith many times. For instance, when they were crossing the lake and the mighty storm blew up (Matthew 8:23–27), Jesus was very clear about asking his disciples why they did not handle the storm themselves. He also asked them, "Where is your faith?" several times in the Gospels (Luke 8:25 and Matthew 14:31). Still, Jesus knew that they had a measure of faith just like you do. The issue is not whether or not we have faith; the issue is, what are we going to do with our faith?

So many times our faith is tested or on trial. God needs us to be strong in faith so that we do not waver when Satan is attacking us in the natural realm. Your wife is cheating. Do you believe that God can restore and renew your marriage? You have been diagnosed with cancer. Do you believe that God can heal you? The curses of this world are not perpetrated by God; they are perpetrated by Satan. It is important to remember that if you are experiencing something that is not in God's promise for your life, then something is amiss. Your first wave of defense is prayer. Praying, when you see any kind of situation contrary to God's word, is so important. God is always asking, "Who are you going to believe, the world or me?" I am here to tell you, faith is a growth process. Faith does not come overnight, unless of course you have the gift of faith. Anyway, you might have to work at this one. I know that before I began my walk with the Lord, I was the biggest pessimist on earth. If it was not sitting before me then I did not believe it was going to happen. "I'll believe it when I see it," that was my motto. I even looked both ways down one-way streets. Now, ask anyone, I believe God will work out every situation. I have even been seen praying healing over my sick children and myself. It is kind of liberating, knowing I don't have to worry about meaningless things anymore because my Father has everything handled. "Speak to the Mountain and it shall be moved" (Matthew 17:20). This is so true because I have seen mountains move in my life and the lives of those I love and it is nothing short of God working through my faith.

When I was diagnosed with cancer I was devastated, but only for a moment. God clearly told me I would have surgery and the cancer would be gone. He revealed this to me even before the oncologist told me what my options were. I received prayer at church, but I knew that this was something I had to go through to strengthen my walk. I am not going to say that fear never crept into my mind. Satan will always come. There were times when I even hoped that this would be the end, and I could be with God, never to endure the trials of my life again. It was a very difficult time for me and my husband. He believed the worst and acted like I was terminal. This disease became an excuse for his behavior. Finally, I had to come to terms with the fact that I was either going to believe God or not. I had to put everything in His hands because trying to deal with this, on top of all of the other things that were going on in my life, really put my faith to the test. I asked God to take everything and carry me through this. God strengthened me, though. He comforted me and let me know that He would be there through every step. He showed me that if I put my faith in Him, He would take care of everything.

Worry set in from time to time. I wondered who would take care of the kids if my husband was unable? Who would take care of me after the surgery? What were we going to do for money while I was out of work? These were questions that plagued me daily, but God showed me that if I believed in Him, He would handle it all. God provided everything just like He said He would. I finally knew that I had faith, and that faith would see me through anything because God is faithful. When I went to the oncologist for a follow-up visit, he told me that they had to check to make sure all the cancer was gone. I remember saying, with confidence, "I know it is all gone." I knew, deep in my heart, that God's word was true, and He said it would be gone, so I knew it was gone.

Note:

Praying properly is very important. If you have faith in God's word and promise, then you know it is not necessary to keep asking for the same things over and over again. His word says "I tell you the truth, my Father will give you whatever you ask in my name" (John 16:23). Not "ask fifteen times on Tuesday and I will let you know by Friday." God is faithful. Ask one time and if what you ask is in line with His word, it is done. After asking, continue to thank Him until you see the physical manifestation of His promise. This can take time, but He may be working out something in you.

Chapter Questions:

Do I understand what faith is?

_____

_____

_____

_____

_____

How can my faith be strengthened?

_____

_____

_____

_____

_____

Scriptures I can use to help me when I need faith

_____

_____

_____

_____

_____

More ways to pray

_____

_____

_____

_____

Notes:

Chapter 6: Prayer for the Beginner

Over and over again I have mentioned praying and reading your Bible. This is mentioned so many times because not only are these some of the strongest tools we are equipped with, they go hand in hand. I know you have, at some point in your life, taken a test and I am pretty sure you prepared in some way. Think of your life as the biggest, most important test you have ever had to take, and there are no retakes, there is no curve; it is simply pass or fail. I really don't think that you want to fail. *Read your word*; do not show up to the fight unprepared. You must know what God has promised you so that you know what to pray. Scripture holds all the information that you need to pray effectively. So, now you may be wondering, "How do I pray? Won't I sound stupid to those around me?" The funny thing is that once you start praying, God works out the rest of the details, and soon others may even be compelled to get involved and pray with you.

> *"Don't show up to the fight unprepared; you have to know what God has promised you so you will know what to pray"*

Now, there are some basic rules to prayer. They are actually very simple, but they must be taken very seriously.

Rule #1: This first rule has pretty much been covered. Read your word. Know your word. I am not saying you need to quote every scripture, but it is imperative that you know what to pray and when to pray it. Just know that not every scripture is meant for every situation. A wise woman once said, "You don't want to use a healing scripture when it is your finances that you are praying about." Learn as many scriptures as you can. Not just the words but what they really mean. You have to get God's word deep on the inside of you so when you speak it, you have the faith that what you have spoken will be done.

Important Scriptures Every New Christian Should Know:

Healing—*By His stripes I am healed* (1 Peter 2:24)

Faith—*Greater is he who is me than he who is in the world* (1 John 4:4)

Perseverance—*For He so loved the world He gave His one and only Son* (John 3:16)

Strength—*My yoke is easy and my burden is light* (Matthew 11:30)

Finances—*Bring the whole tithe into the storehouse, that there may be food in my house. Test me in this, says the LORD Almighty, and see if I will not throw open the* floodgates *of heaven and pour out so much blessing that you will not have room enough for it* (Malachi 3:10)

Rule #2: Don't be afraid to pray anywhere. Prayer strengthens your relationship with God. Kind of how long phone calls strengthen your relationship with someone you have just started dating. Those conversations are important because you both have to learn about each other and develop trust and a bond. Anyone who has had a new relationship knows what this is like. Think about it: the amount of time you spend getting to know your new love interest usually reflects how serious you are about the relationship. How serious is your relationship with God? Now, if you are afraid to talk on the phone in front of other people, the person you are dating may take offense. "Why are you keeping me a secret?" It works the same with your Father. He wants you to be excited to speak to Him. Pray in your car, in your home, and even pray over your food in the lunchroom or in a restaurant. You can no longer worry that others may think you are different, so now you have to act like you are different. In fact Jesus addresses this very clearly by saying, "But whoever disowns me before men, I will disown him before my Father in heaven" in Matthew 10:33.

Rule #3: In addition to praying anywhere and everywhere, you will also need to have a special, private place to pray. You will understand why as you grow up in the Spirit. Just know that some prayer is between you and God alone, and the Holy Spirit can help you effectively and deeply pray if you remove distractions and focus solely on God.

7 Prayer Rules for the Beginner

Rule #4: "One can set 1,000 to flight, but 2 can set 10,000 to flight" (Deuteronomy 32:30). You have already learned that there is strength in numbers, and having one or two other people to pray with can only increase the effectiveness of your prayers. God does not ask us to go through this life on our own and he will place people in our midst if we ask him to. Just remember, prayer is for you, God, and others, so don't be stingy; spread the prayer. An important point to mention is that it is our responsibility to guard our mind, body, and spirit. Be wary of people praying for you who may not have your best interest at heart. Through prayer you will learn what the Holy Spirit sounds like, and it is not necessary for you to allow just anyone to speak over your life. I know this sounds a little paranoid, but we have to be careful and guard the gifts that the Holy Father has placed in us; not everyone is on His mission.

Rule #5: Speak those things that be not as though they were (Romans 4:17). Speak about the situation as if it has already manifested for your eyes to see. Once you pray for it, it is done! We ask once and then we thank God for the work He has done, even if we do not see the manifestation yet. It says so clearly in the word to ask and it shall be given unto you (Luke 11:9). As you will learn, in this book, your words can bring life or death. When we pray we are directly connected to God; He hears you. "Daddy, can I have a cookie? Daddy, can I have a cookie? Daddy …" Every parent knows how annoying that is, and our Father is not any different. We can remind Him of His promises, but it is not necessary to keep asking Him for the same things over and over again. You have to have faith that God answers prayers and He loves each and every one of His children equally.

Rule #6: Keep track of your prayers and the results. An affirmation list is a wonderful tool that will allow you to see God working. Often we pray for things and then after we receive them we are tempted to write it off as common or explainable outside of God. For example, say you are praying for a new car. You get the car and after a while Satan begins to convince you that you got that car because you paid off your bills and raised your credit score. Or for some of you, because the sales guy thought you were really cute in those boots and worked extra hard for you, whatever lie Satan would have you to believe. Now, God has been removed from the equation and He has not received the glory for His work. Big mistake; all glory should go to God. Make a list of the things you are praying and believing for, and then write dates and notes next to those things when God answers your prayers. Do not throw the list away. Keep it for a rainy day when you need to be reminded of how good He is to you.

Rule #7: Don't make promises you just can't keep. It's a classic rookie mistake. Making vows is very clearly prohibited in Matthew 5:36–37, which reads, "and do not swear by your head, for you cannot make even one hair white or black." Promising God that if He gives you a million dollars, you will give half to the church is not going to work. He knows you and He has seen you work. Unless the Caribbean is a secret Church of God, you are not planning to give anything away to anybody. God will never place more on you than you can bear. This includes the things that we may want, but are totally unprepared to have. Be obedient with the thousand He gave you on your tax return and show Him you can be trusted with more. You do not have to bargain with God and you certainly do not have to make any promises that the both of you know are untrue. Be honest with yourself and Him. When you do this He will honor your prayers.

When my husband and I were first together, I was a believer but not a Christian. I did not endeavor to walk as Christ walked, not yet. My husband also believed in God, but he did not actively walk with Christ either. At this point, you could say that we were evenly yoked. I had a desire to learn more about God, and my husband had expressed his desire to stay in the place that he was. I believe he even told me, at one point, he "talked to God, and God knew his heart and that was good enough." Over the years he began to feel the same way I did, that something was missing. He met an old friend one day, and decided that we would join him for Bible study. We went to Bible study three times a week for about five months and during this time our marriage began to deteriorate. We prayed at the beginning and the end of the study, but it was always lacking; it felt like there was no power in it. My husband was battling demons that, quite frankly, the people we were studying with were unable to teach us how to fight effectively. I couldn't tell everyone what I was going through because I felt that we would be judged and I did not want that. I felt hopeless and alone. It was clear that I had not yet learned how to have a relationship with God.

After a huge blowout at home, I was walking to the bank. While I was walking, one of my close friends called and I could not even contain the hurt, anger, and frustration. Immediately, she called her pastor's wife. They dropped everything and prayed with me, right there, on the phone. I didn't know this woman from Adam, and she was willing to take the time to pray with me, someone who she did not even know. This is what I have been looking for; this is what I needed. My friend stepped in and did what she knew to do, pray and ask God to take care of the situation. The prayer was powerful and I felt like things would change. I knew, at that moment, that God had sent me to people who would care for me and my family. My husband was not as receptive to our new church family. He did not want to attend church with me and he really did not want me taking time out of our lives to be there either. There were arguments that directly correlated with my church attendance. It became a difficult situation for me. However, I knew that I had to do this for me, for us. I had to be around people who knew how to be Christians. People who knew God intimately and were not reserved about sharing what they know. People experienced in prayer and all that it had to offer. Now, there are four of us who pray every morning and any other time that one of us or our church family is in need. We are all there for each other to offer support when one is down, to offer Godly wisdom, and sometimes just to be present through a situation. We have seen our prayers come to manifestation and that is a great gift.

Chapter Questions:

Who can I pray with?

_____

_____

_____

_____

_____

Where can I pray privately?

_____

_____

_____

_____

_____

When can I pray during the day?

_____

_____

_____

_____

_____

Affirmation list

_____

_____

_____

_____

_____

_____

_____

_____

_____

Scriptures that will help me to pray effectively

_____

_____

_____

_____

_____

_____

_____

_____

Notes:

Chapter 7: Find Your Purpose

God has given each and every one of us spiritual gifts and He requires us to use these gifts to further advance His Kingdom. The fruits of the Spirit are "love, joy, peace, patience, kindness, goodness, faithfulness, gentleness and self-control" (Galatians 5:22–23).

The gifts of the Spirit are found in 1 Corinthians 7–10: "Now to each one the manifestation of the Spirit is given for the common good. To one there is given through the Spirit the message of wisdom, to another the message of knowledge by means of the same Spirit, to another faith by the same Spirit, to another gifts of healing by that one Spirit, to another miraculous powers, to another prophecy, to another distinguishing between spirits, to another speaking in different kinds of tongues, and to still another the interpretation of tongues."

> "Everyone has a purpose and Satan will try to pervert it and use it in the world."

Is there something that you are good at, maybe even excellent? Chances are this is one of your spiritual gifts that God intended for His Kingdom and that Satan has perverted for the world. Let's say that you are a singer, Karaoke queen or king. You know every word to every song that Beyoncé ever made and you are good. You sound just like her. Unfortunately, Sony Records missed your demo tape and you are just sitting here until you are discovered. Now, suppose you took that gift for song and used it for the Kingdom of God. I have experienced this firsthand and I have to tell you, say Beyoncé times ten. God will use your gift for His Glory and it will touch people.

Maybe your gift is not so cut and dried. God puts things in our hearts, and we are the ones who miss the prompts. How many people go to church every Sunday for one hour, mingle for ten minutes, and then go back home? Is this the impact that God talks about in the Bible? How are we going to advance the Kingdom of God sitting in front of Monday night reruns? If you want to be an effective member of the Kingdom of God, then it is your responsibility to discover your purpose and then walk in that purpose. There are many stories in the Bible that involve people who hear from God and then act on His word. There are also those, like Jonah for instance, who try to run from what the Lord has for them, only to find out His will must always be done.

My suggestion is to pray about this. Ask God to reveal your purpose and then show you the path you need to take to walk in that purpose. Are you supposed to be an usher or a praise team member? Perhaps you have been called to teach Sunday school or dance? Maybe you are a prayer warrior or even a prophet? How will you know if you do not ask? Asking is not the end of your journey, though. You must begin to walk in your purpose, to begin finding ways to fulfill the position that God has for you. If you are not sure about what God has for you, then it is okay to ask someone you trust for some additional guidance on how to pray. After all, this is something that is new to you and asking for help can sometimes be very intimidating.

Another important thing to remember is that God has a marvelous plan for your life, and that plan probably includes many steps. What you have been led to do today may not be the thing that you will be walking in five years from now. You must be willing to change and grow as God sees fit. You may have been counting the offering money only to prepare you for future work on the fund-raising committee. I understand that change can be a frightening thing and Satan would have you believing all sorts of lies about your Godly purpose. He will whisper in your ear, telling you that you are not good enough or you are trying to be something you are not. Resist the devil and he will flee, remember? God has chosen you for a reason and God does not make mistakes. You must be willing to see the potential that He has placed in you.

Earlier, I was telling you that I began fulfilling my purpose in the church by singing. After about six months of singing back up, I was pushed into the role of worship leader. This is not where I really wanted to be, but I knew that if God wanted this from me then it was my obligation to follow through. With the leadership came prayer, and this is when things started getting sticky. I remember the first time I prayed alone with my pastor's wife, regarding my husband. I should preempt this by telling you that I am not really a fighter. I try to avoid physical conflict because I feel it is not the most effective way to solve problems. As I was praying with my pastor's wife, all of a sudden, the Holy Spirit overcame me and I was in the midst of a battle. I could see swords flying and devastating damage was being inflicted on the enemy. I could see everything like it was happening right in front of me. The two of us ended the prayer session in awe of what had just happened. I couldn't really remember exactly what I said, but I knew that the message was an attack against whatever was coming to disrupt me and my family. Later, I found out that I have a warring spirit; that when I pray, I have the capability to be on the offensive regarding Satan and his cohorts. This was a huge surprise because I didn't even know it existed and I certainly did not know how to use it; honestly, I was a little afraid of it. I placed this on the backburner and only allowed it to manifest occasionally.

My role was changing in the church. I began taking the praise and worship very seriously, a little too seriously. When people weren't getting involved I was offended and compelled to help them understand that they were missing out on something great. This created distraction. Finally, I decided I had to focus on my worship with God and not everyone else's. Eventually, I felt disdain for the whole worship service. I was just going through the motions, but I liked having a job in the ministry. After some time, it was time for me to step down. I did not want this—at first, in fact, I took it very personally—but this was because I had never told anyone that I believed this was my purpose and once you have a purpose that is it, end of story, you will be doing that for the rest of your life. What my pastor later revealed to me is that what I was feeling was the separation of the anointing. When I began singing, it was what I needed at the time and what God needed from me, so I was anointed to do it. This period had been a time for growth, but now I needed to move on to the next thing that God had for me. I began to understand that I could be an effective prayer and this would be something that I would have to develop and learn how to use. I also began helping with the structure and background of the church. God started using me in my new roles because He has a plan for my life. This book was part of His plan and there is more to come. I am now open for every assignment and eager to show Him I am His willing and faithful servant.

Chapter Questions:

What is my purpose?

_____

_____

_____

How would God like to use me?

_____

_____

_____

_____

Try this prayer:

Father please lead me and guide me to my purpose. My desire is to please You and walk in what You would have for me. Father please show me clearly so that I know how to proceed in this position that you have for me. Lord God, I am a willing vessel to do Your work and advance Your Kingdom. Thank You for your love and guidance.

My purpose is:

_____

_____

_____

Answers I received from God

_____

_____

_____

_____

Steps I will take to begin walking in my purpose

_____

_____

_____

_____

_____

_____

Notes:

_____
_____
_____
_____
_____
_____
_____
_____
_____
_____
_____
_____
_____
_____
_____
_____
_____
_____
_____
_____
_____
_____
_____
_____
_____
_____
_____
_____
_____

Chapter 8: Forgive Who?

Have you ever been driving and then been cut off? Let me ask you: what did speeding up to the guy and flipping the bird really solve? What did stewing about it all day really accomplish? Please tell me you didn't talk about it with the people at work. You really let some driver get into your head like that? Well, that is kind of the way unforgiveness works. The more time you spend stewing over the wrongs someone has committed against you, the

> "Everyone has a purpose and Satan will try to pervert it and use it in the world."

more of *your* time and energy you have wasted. Think about it: who does unforgiveness hurt? Do you really think that your ex is sitting up in her apartment with her new boyfriend thinking about how much you hate her? No, while you are spending time with your friends plotting and planning her demise, she is living her life and you are wasting yours. Why give anyone that much control over your life?

Actually, I learned about forgiveness before I was trying to live saved. My ex-husband had been previously married. His ex-wife hated him and everything about him. Every time they would get on the phone, to talk about the kids, they always ended up in the same place, an angry hang-up. I never heard both sides of the conversation fully but I got the gist of most of her animosity because I could hear the screaming through the phone. She was angry with him still and they had not been together for years. To make matters worse, she was in a new relationship. I observed how her anger and hatred affected her and her new relationship. She was bitter and refused to forgive and let everything go. I swore, from that moment on, that I would never let anyone have that much control over me, especially if we were no longer together.

I have had to forgive others for verbal and physical abuse, adultery, and just plain horrible treatment, which would take a few pages in itself to describe. Forgiving is not an easy thing to do and it is never instant. Do I still try to have amicable relationships with my exes? Yes. The fact that we have children together gives me all the more reason to put the past behind me and get on with the future. Satan would love to see us eaten up with the anger and resentment that unforgiveness harbors. He wants us to lash out at the people who cause us harm; this makes his job easier. I refused to let him get the best of me. I knew God could change my heart in any situation and help me to forgive everyone in my life. I let Him take the unforgiveness and turn it into love and compassion for others, even if they did not return this to me. Forgiveness is liberating and it helps you more than it helps them.

But the things that so and so did are horrendous! Personally, I have been through some things that people only have nightmares about, and if I can forgive, so can you. I am not saying you have to have makeover parties with the people who have wronged you, but forgive them. Some things may be harder to forgive than others but it is important, in your walk with God, to be able to forgive. Don't get me wrong, it may take time to forgive. You may have to really pray about it, but you must make it your goal to forgive everyone; otherwise, how can you expect God to forgive you?

I mean God sent His only son to die for you and your sins, so you should take it personally. He forgave you before you were even born, so who are you to deny forgiveness? In His word it states that unless you forgive, you won't be forgiven, and that this forgiveness must be from the heart (Matthew 18:23–35). This is a command to forgive or you will suffer the consequences. I am reminded of the story about the servant who was forgiven of his debt in Matthew 18:23–35.

The story reads, "Therefore, the kingdom of heaven is like a king who wanted to settle accounts with his servants. As he began the settlement, a man who owed him ten thousand talents was brought to him. Since he was not able to pay, the master ordered that he and his wife and his children and all that he had be sold to repay the debt. The servant fell on his knees before him. 'Be patient with me,' he begged, 'and I will pay back everything.' The servant's master took pity on him, canceled the debt and let him go. "But when that servant went out, he found one of his fellow servants who owed him a hundred denarii. He grabbed him and began to choke him. 'Pay back what you owe me!' he demanded. His fellow servant fell to his knees and begged him, 'Be patient with me, and I will pay you back.' But he refused. Instead, he went off and had the man thrown into prison until he could pay the debt. When the other servants saw what had happened, they were greatly distressed and went and told their master everything that had happened. Then the master called the servant in. 'You wicked servant,' he said, 'I canceled all that debt of yours because you begged me to. Shouldn't you have had mercy on your fellow servant just as I had on you?' In anger his master turned him over to the jailers to be tortured, until he should pay back all he owed. This is how my heavenly Father will treat each of you unless you forgive your brother from your heart."

Don't be that servant. Pray that God will help you to forgive. Now, I am not saying to forget. Wisdom comes out of learning from these lifelong learning experiences. For example, if your best friend steals money out of your purse, don't forgive him or her and then leave your purse in their lap while you go to the bathroom. That would be foolish. Use these experiences to learn and become wiser.

Chapter Questions:

Who do I need to forgive?

_____

_____

_____

_____

Who do I need forgiveness from?

_____

_____

_____

_____

How can I pray for those who hate me?

_____

_____

_____

_____

_____

_____

Notes:

Chapter 9: Watch Your Mouth

Believe it or not, your mouth is a powerful weapon. It has the power to bring of life or death. "The tongue has the power of life and death, and those who love it will eat its fruit" is how it is stated in the word (Proverbs 18:21). Have you ever heard someone say that you would never amount to anything? Or maybe these were your words to someone else. God has given words power and what we say will come to pass, so if this works for good it also works for evil. I know that when someone ticks you off your first response is to get back at them. Sometimes this retaliation is physical and sometimes all it takes is your words. Has anyone ever said anything to you that hurt you? How about anything that made you question who you are? Have you ever wondered why? Because words have power; there is no other way to say it.

Now you know that it is important for you to begin with a clean slate. God can redeem you from every negative word that has come out of your mouth and every word that has been spoken against you. Here is a prayer to help you with this;

Lord, I repent from any negative word I have spoken against others both knowingly and unknowingly, I ask that you put a guard on my mouth and purpose the Holy Spirit to only allow goodness to flow hereafter. In addition I ask for protection from any negative thing that has been spoken against me. I am a child of the Most High God and I curse any words that suggested I will be anything less, Amen.

Here are some tools that will help you to guard your mouth. First of all, fill yourself with God's word and try to eliminate as much of the world from your daily life as possible. Next, think before you speak, and as always, if you don't have anything nice to say, don't say anything at all (Thanks, Mom).

I have seen the power of our words work in both directions. The words we utter are powerful tools that cause things to manifest. One day, my husband and I were talking about our oldest son. The two of them had not been getting along and they were constantly fighting. Our son did not agree with some of the choices that my husband was making, and this led to argument after argument. When my husband and I were talking, he sarcastically stated that he hoped our son would never have to deal with the issues that he had had to deal with because that was where our son was headed. I did not curse the words against my son as I should have and less than a year later, a child who had no history of drug interaction was being put on probation and entering rehab. I believe that this situation was spoken into existence and the entire situation could have been averted if the words had not been negative.

The flip side of the coin occurred last year when we were waiting on our tax refund. We submitted our return using the E-file so that it would come back quickly. Our federal return went through smoothly. Our state return was another story. It had been selected for a random review. I logged onto the state Web site and looked at the information they gave regarding the potential processing date. It was in July, which was six months away. That date was unacceptable; we needed that money to pay some bills off. I prayed about the situation and asked God to move in the situation. Then I proceeded to write a date on the calendar. The date was the last Friday in February. After that, I spoke the date out of my mouth and declared that the money would be in our account by this specific date. I checked the site about a week before my spoken date and nothing had changed. It still read July for processing. The last Friday in February, I was checking our account and there was a deposit; our state refund had been deposited on the precise day that I had proclaimed. The power of my words and my faith in God's devotion to me and my family produced a manifestation of large proportions. It was glorious watching God move. Our words can bring life or death and we need to choose wisely.

After we have accepted Jesus into our heart, we are now given the ability to be filled by the Holy Spirit. Why not take advantage? If you are dealing with a situation that is causing you to think some negative things, pray about it. Ask the Holy Spirit to guide you. Watch what you speak out of your mouth. Do you really want your husband to be a good-for-nothing drunk like his father? Then why would you speak it? Is little Johnny really the spitting image of his womanizing Uncle Frank? You might want to rethink the family resemblance before you speak it out of your mouth. Oh, and before I forget, stop speaking negative into your situation. Do you really want to be broke? Then maybe you should think before you say you are broke. This goes for other things as well, like "cancer runs in my family" or "I will never get the job." Do you see any familiar phrases that may have cursed your own situation? "My dear brothers, take note of this: Everyone should be quick to listen, slow to speak, and slow to become angry" (James 1:19). Remember, life or death is all in the power of your tongue; be very careful how you use it (Proverbs 14:29).

Chapter Questions:

Have I prayed the prayer of repentance?

_____

_____

How can I stop speaking curses and death into my life and the lives of others?

_____

_____

_____

_____

Can I count to ten before speaking in any situation?

_____

_____

What can I pray before speaking?

_____

_____

_____

Notes:

Chapter 10: End of the Beginning

So, there you have it. These are all things that I wish I knew when I started my walk. As a parent I want my children to be able to learn from the mistakes I made so that they do not have to repeat them. I want the same for you. If the tools in this book help you to become closer to God, than I am glad I bumped my head time and time again. Use these tools and suggestions, build upon them, and make your walk with God into something meaningful and lifelong.

> *Please use this as a tool to build a meaningful relationship with God.*

I hope you have picked up your Bible and found some verses that will help you. It is also my prayer that you have taken some notes and begun to really understand what God means to you and how amazing this walk can be. Share God with your family and friends. They will see the changes in you. Just don't ever be discouraged if they do not accept the changes. Remember, even Jesus could not perform miracles in His hometown because they did not see him as a child of God; they saw him as a child of man and this kept them from having faith (Mark 6:4–6). You are now on your way to becoming everything God has for you to be. There will be more books to come. As I learn I will be sure to share with you because I know that God wants us all to be successful.

Don't ever give up! By now you have probably been getting

stronger. You have come so far, I know it, and you have so much further to go. Remember, God loves you with an unconditional love that we humans can't even comprehend. If you fall, get up, dust yourself off, and keep pressing forward. I can't even count the number of times I have missed the mark, but the true test is whether or not you will get up and try again. This is the only way to succeed. One final note to consider: if this walk were easy, everyone would do it.

Dedication

All the Glory to God for the words that are in these pages. As You have told me what to write, I pray that I have done it justice in Your eyes. Also, Heavenly Father, I would like to thank you for the people you have placed in my life. To my beloved children, thank you for loving me no matter what; no words can describe the love I feel for each of you. Mom and Dad, thanks for always being there for me. To the people who have helped me to make it through so many storms: My Living Word family and my best friends C, D, T, and S. I love every one of you and thank you for standing by my side through it all.

Essential Terms for the Beginner

Agape Love—Agape love is the type of love exhibited by Jesus Christ. It's a love that's given and expects no return.

Baptism—The application of water to a person, as a sacrament or religious ceremony, by which he or she is initiated into the visible church of Christ. This is performed by immersion, sprinkling, or pouring.

Bible—The collection of sacred writings of the Christian religion, comprising the Old and New Testaments.

Burden—That which is borne with difficulty; obligation.

Holy Spirit—In the belief of many Christians, one of the three persons in the one God, along with the Father (God) and the Son (Jesus); the Holy Spirit is also called the Holy Ghost. Jesus promised the Apostles that he would send the Holy Spirit after his Crucifixion and Resurrection. The Spirit came to the disciples of Jesus on Pentecost.

Jesus—A teacher and prophet whose life and teachings form the basis of Christianity. Christians believe Jesus to be Son of God and the Christ.

Obedience—Words or actions denoting submission to authority; dutifulness.

Patience—An ability or willingness to suppress restlessness or annoyance when confronted with delay.

Perseverance—Steady persistence in a course of action, a purpose, a state, and so on, especially in spite of difficulties, obstacles, or discouragement.

Prayer—Spiritual communion with God, sometimes as an act of worship, as in supplication, thanksgiving, adoration, or confession.

Prophets—A person chosen by God to speak to and guide the people of Israel. Moses was the greatest of the Old Testament prophets.

Satan—The profoundly evil adversary of God and humanity, often identified as the leader of the fallen angels; the Devil.

Submission—The act of yielding to power or authority.

Wisdom—Knowledge of what is true or right coupled with just judgment as to action.

Yoke—In biblical terms, something that couples or binds together; a bond or tie. The name was derived from the device that binds draught animals together.

Christian Terms Glossary

Terms That Every Christian Should Know:

Accountability— In the Bible we are instructed that we have a choice in everything, but we will be held responsible for our actions. Some choose to blame Satan for all their problems when there is evidence that suggests that because we make poor choices, we bring about many problems in our own lives.

Apostle—Christians are apostles or messengers of God's word. It is our job to share His word with those that do not know Him.

Blasphemy—People achieve blasphemy by publicly discounting or denying God's word. Blasphemy of the Holy Spirit is the only unforgivable sin according to God's word.

Confess—Confessing is an action and it means to declare or admit. One can confess sins to God for forgiveness and healing. One can also proclaim or confess his faith when he is witnessing about God to others.Covenant— A covenant is a pact or bonding agreement between two or more parties. In Christianity we have a covenant with God through Jesus and that covenant is strengthened through things like fasting, prayer and communion.

Disciple—A disciple is a direct follower or student of Jesus. The gospels were written by some of the disciples of Christ.

Epistle—This is a letter that is used in the New Testament to inform people of the teachings of Jesus and God. Paul wrote many epistles included in the books of: Romans, Corinthians and Ephesians.

Grace—Grace is God's undying love and devotion to His children, us. He has given this to us without our having to earn it through deeds or acts.

Holy Spirit—The Holy Spirit is part of God's trinity. He dwells within God's children. The Holy Spirit leads and guides us to do the right thing in God, like a Holy conscience. He descended upon Jesus when Jesus was baptized and now He exists in us after we accept Jesus as our Lord and Savior.

Lamb of God—In the Old Testament lambs were sacrificed to remove sin from God's people. Jesus is the Lamb of God that was sacrificed for all of our sins. He willingly gave His son so that we do not have to die in sin.

Lord's Supper or Communion—Before Jesus was sacrificed He performed a final supper with His disciples. This was a profound occasion in which He compared the wine to His blood and the bread to His body. Communion consists of wine and bread that is taken by God's children in order to become closer to Him through the remembrance of His sacrifice.

Patriarch—A patriarch is a father or male head of a family. Abraham was told by God that He would father countless offspring making him a patriarch of many Hebrew nations.

Pentecost— This is a feast celebrated , by the Jews, after Passover. Christians celebrate this in reference to Christ's sacrifice on the cross symbolizing the arrival of the Holy Spirit in Christians.

Pharisee— These are followers of the law given to Moses by God. The Pharisees refused to accept change when Jesus eliminated the old laws and implemented redemption for all of our sins through His crucifixion. Pharisees had issues with some of the things Jesus did like healing on the Sabbath and forgiving sins like adultery without stoning. They were constantly questioning Jesus and His behavior.

Reconcile—Reconciliation is the restoration of relationships. Jesus brought us closer to God with His crucifixion and reconciled our relationship with our father.

Redemption— This is the price that Jesus paid for our souls. He redeemed our lives when he was crucified on the cross.

Repent—When we repent it means that we turn away and it is generally used in reference to sin. God forgives us of all things (excluding blasphemy of the Holy Spirit) but when we repent we show Him that we are truly sorry for what we have done and willing to make an effort not to commit the same sin over and over again.

Resurrection—It was necessary for His flesh to die, His spirit to descend into hell and then His spirit to rise again to His place by His father. This is what eliminated our need to go to hell. It also gave us a direct pathway to God.

Salvation—Salvation is the eternal life given to us by Jesus' sacrifice. Salvation takes away our sins and allows us to be new in God.

Sin—Sin is the wrong that separates us from God. Our fleshly bodies are immersed in Sin and as Christians we have to strive to eliminate sin from our lives.

Witness—In an accident situation a witness is someone who tells their view of the accident. In God a witness is someone who brings forth God's word to others. It is the duty of all Christian's to be witnesses of God's word and goodness.

LaVergne, TN USA
05 November 2009
163097LV00001B/110/P